Let's Take Care of Our New Cat

Núria Roca / Rosa M. Curto

BARRON'S

Should we adopt a cat?

The family that lives next door to Pete and Paula is looking for a family who would like to adopt a kitten. Their cat had five kittens in her litter!

The kittens are now two months old, so they may be separated from their mother.

Guess who offers to take care of one of the kittens forever and ever?

First day at home

The first day the kitten gets home, they leave him in a room. He has a comfortable cushion, a food bowl, a water bowl, and a litter box.

Pete and Paula keep him company and caress him so he will not miss his brothers and sisters so much. They also give him a name: Rufus!

A big responsibility

Rufus gets used to his new home very quickly. He knows his food bowl and his water bowl are kept in the kitchen, and the litter box where he has to "do his thing" is in the utility room.

The children are in charge of keeping the cat's things nice and clean and making sure he always has fresh water. Taking care of a cat takes a lot of work!

His own things

Collar

Flea collar

Bowls

Nail cutter

Oil

Hair patter

Brush

Soap

Comb

Mitten

Bug repellent

Pooper scoop

Kitty litter

Litter box

Cotton swabs

Toy duster

Travel bag

Pillow

Play tunnel

Snacks

SNAKS

Ball toy

Bed

Scratching post

Travel case

Toy mice

Very independent

Rufus loves being with Pete and Paula, but sometimes he doesn't feel like playing. In these cases, the best thing they can do is leave him alone.

Cats are not toys and they often enjoy being on their own.

I love being bored!

I am always experimenting
with things that are new
to me.

I enjoy playing
with balls of yarn.

Like cats and dogs!

At Rufus' new home there is also a puppy, so the childrens' parents decide to introduce them. Do you think they will fight?
First they watch one another from a distance. After a while they get close enough to sniff and smell each other. They are more willing to play than fight!

Claws and teeth

Rufus still has to learn how to play without hurting anyone. When he is in a playful mood, he sticks out his nails and bites with his very sharp teeth.

Pete never shouts at him, and never hits him. He just says "No!" in a loud, clear voice and stops playing with him. This way, Rufus will learn that there will be no playing if he bites or scratches.

Visiting the veterinarian

Today the kitten will go to the veterinarian for the first time.
Paula takes Rufus out of his travel cage and holds him in a
way that leaves his hind legs hanging.

   The veterinarian shows her how to hold the cat correctly:
put a hand on the cat's chest going around his front legs,
and put your other hand under the cat's hind legs.

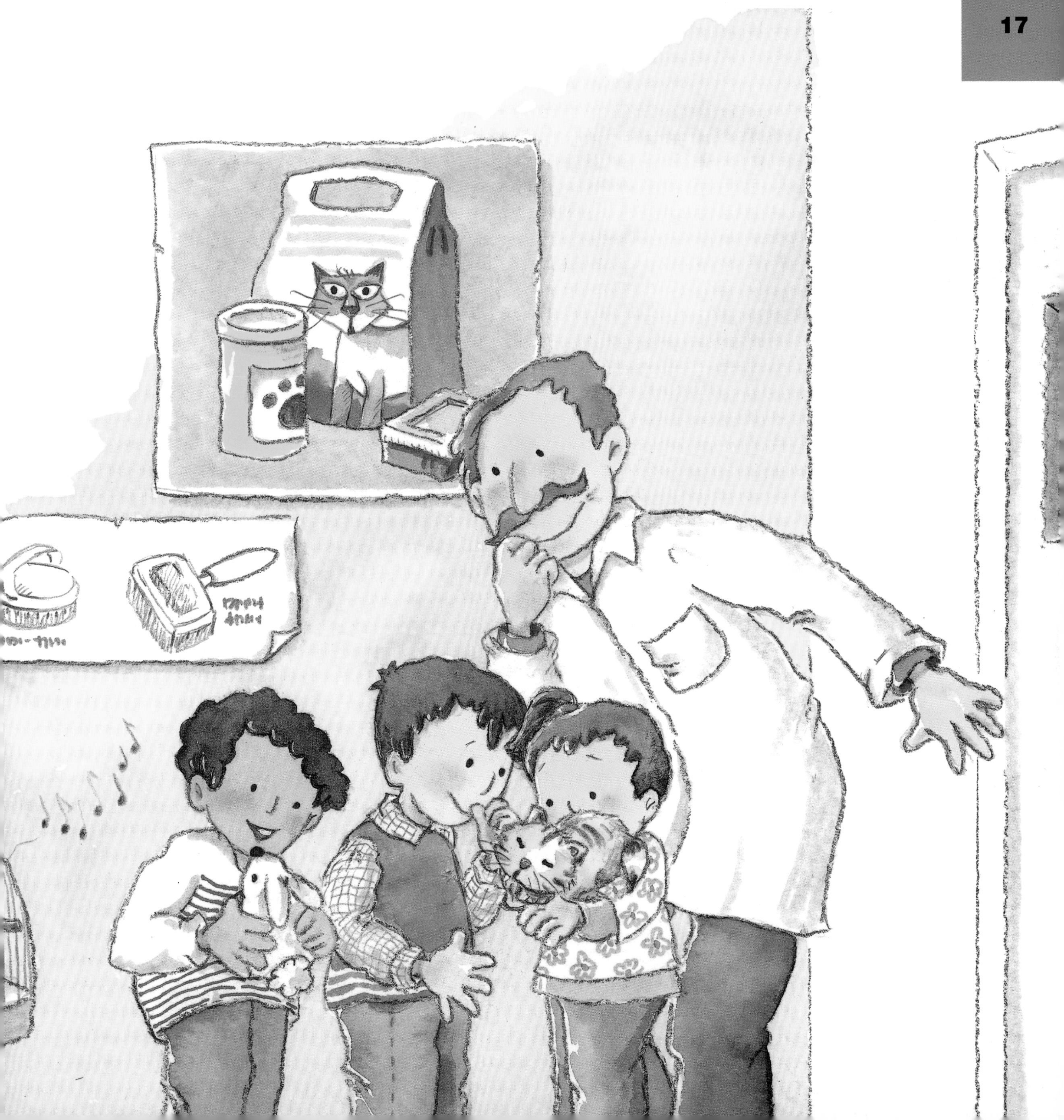

Traveling

When Rufus is in the car, he is always kept inside his travel cage, which is placed in the back seat between Paula and Pete.

Can you imagine what would happen if they carried him in their arms? If he felt scared for any reason, he would try to escape!

Everyone in the car would have a hard time—the cat, the children, and the parents!

Catnip

When Rufus licks himself, he swallows a lot of his own hairs and sometimes he gets a ball of fur in his stomach. Apparently, eating grass is a good way for him to get rid of them.

The childrens' parents have put away all plants that could be poisonous to the cat so he will not eat them. Instead, they have planted a special kind of weed called catnip that cats like very much.

Filing my nails

Wild cats scratch trees to sharpen their claws and to mark their territory. They don't like company very much.

Rufus has no trees near his home, so he has decided the sofa might be a good substitute. Fortunately, the family had already bought a scratching post.

"You may only sharpen your claws here," Pete teaches him.

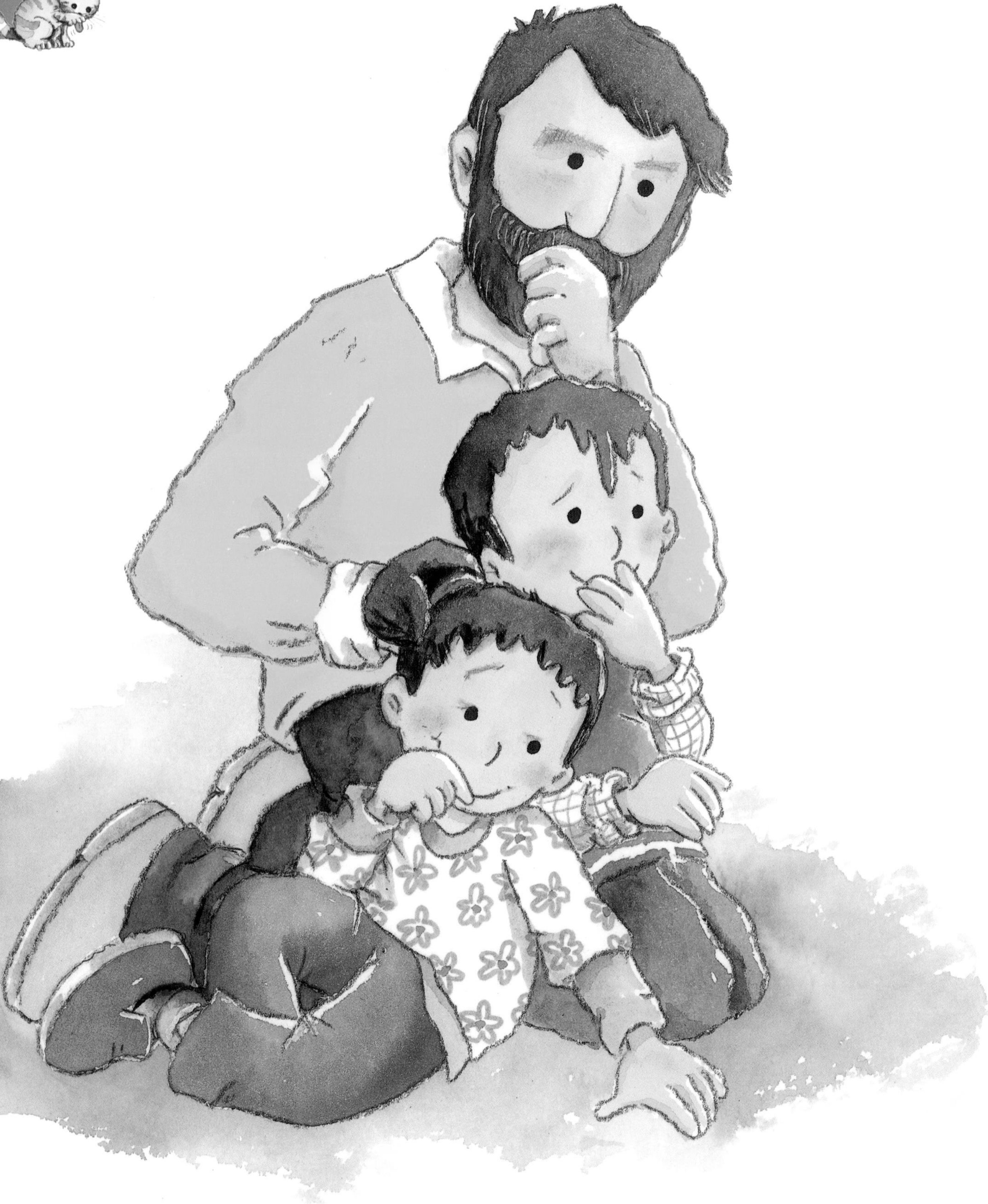

Bon appétit!

Pete and Paula are in charge of feeding the kitten, and they buy cat food at a specialty pet store. They choose a good quality, premium cat food that has everything the kitten needs for a good diet like beef, fish, and vegetables. With this kind of food, he will grow up to be strong and healthy.

Paula didn't know that besides beef, cats also need to eat vegetables to grow nice and healthy, just like children do.

Cat language

When a cat is afraid, he flattens his ears back and curls up in a ball, very close to the ground.

When he is angry, he arches his back, his hair stands on end, he shows his claws, and he even hisses!

When he is happy, can you guess what he does?

I am scared.

Watch out, or I'll scratch you!

I love rolling around!

My favorite
pastime:
sleeping!

At times I love
to meow.

I love to play with
insects ...

... with leaves
blowing in the
wind ...

... or anything that moves.
I love to play!

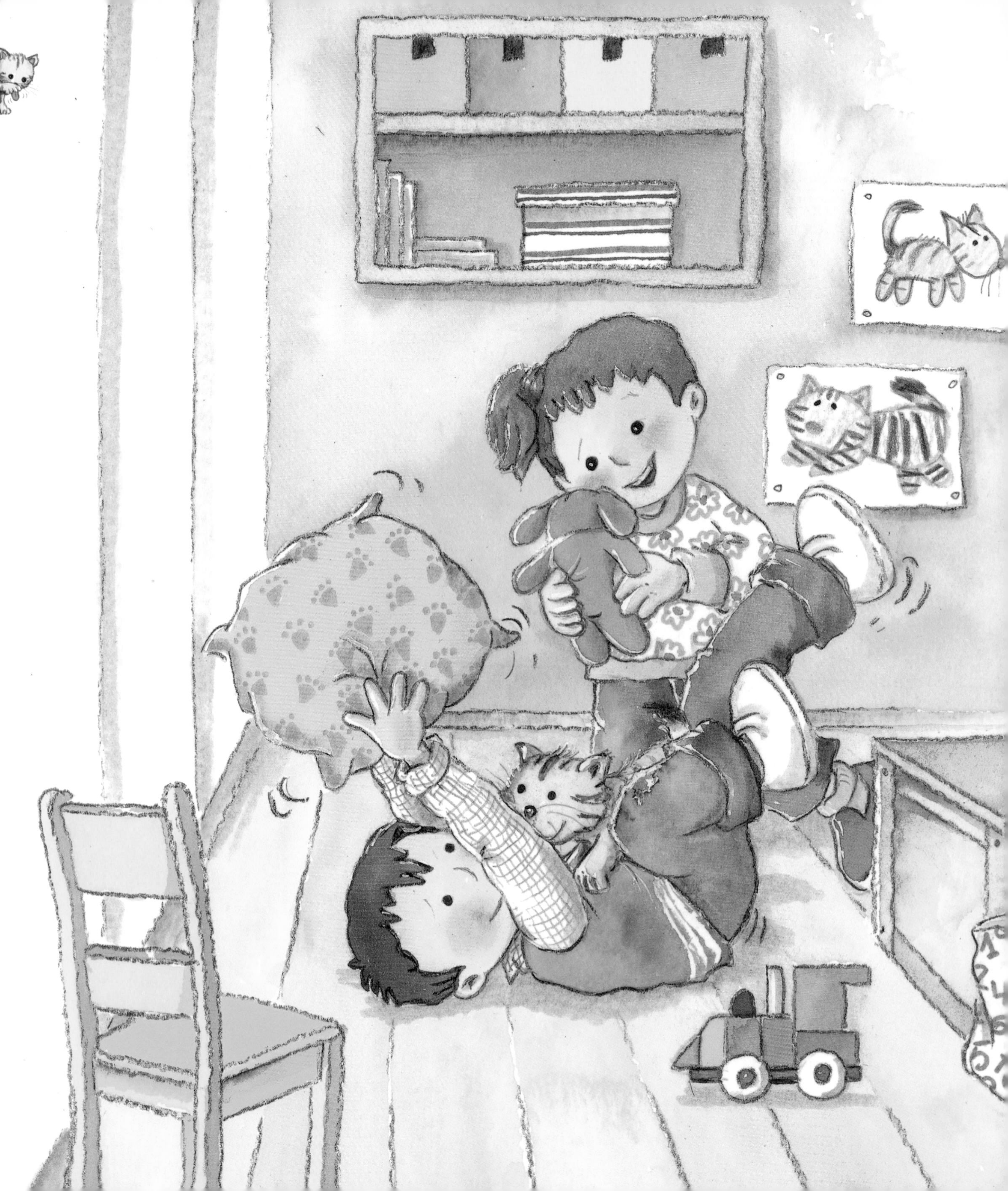

A tiger at home

When Rufus hears his name called, he runs toward the person calling him. Do you know how they taught him his name? By calling him over for nice things, such as feeding or petting.

Paula and Pete love watching him walk toward them. He looks like a small tiger who is delighted to be at home.

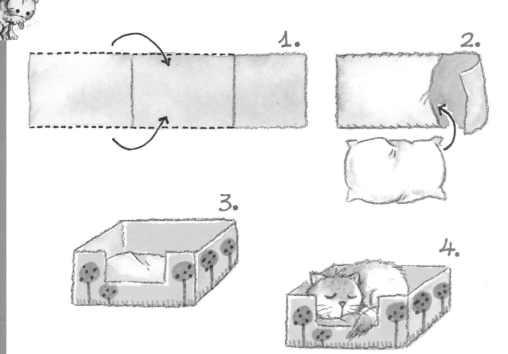

1.

2.

3.

4.

MAKING A BED

Wouldn't it be nice to have your kitten sleep in a bed that you made? You just need a cardboard box, some markers, a sewing needle, some thread, some fabric, and a pillow.

First, make a pillowcase. You will be able to remove the case and wash it whenever it gets dirty. Ask your parents to cut up the fabric to fit the pillow, following the template in the illustration.

Fold the fabric as shown and sew the dotted sides together. There! Now you have a pillowcase.

Now prepare the box. Cut it as shown in the illustration, paint it as you like, and place the pillow inside. Your kitten may now go to sleep!

A TOY

You can make a very simple toy for your kitten. You just need a long rubber band and a bottle cork.

1. Tie the rubber band to the cork, wrapping it very tightly.
2. Hang the rubber band from any door handle and put the cork at a height your kitten can reach.
3. Knock on the door to call your kitten and show him how the cork jumps and swings. He'll be playing with it in no time!

After a while, take the toy away and hide it so your kitten will not lose interest in his new toy.

Activities

Guidelines from the veterinarian

HOW KITTENS GROW

Have you decided to adopt a kitten? Well then, how about learning a few things about them? When kittens are between 7 and 10 days old, they open their eyes but they aren't able to see very well yet. When they are 2–3 weeks old, they start walking and when they are 3 weeks old, they learn from their mother how to use a litter box.

Until they are 4 weeks old, their hearing is not completely developed. When they are 4–5 weeks old, they should start running. When they are a month and a half old, they already have all their milk (or baby) teeth.

When they are about 8 weeks old, even though they may seem too small, the kittens are ready to be separated from their mother. They can now go and live with a human family!

BEING WELL INFORMED

Kittens, like children, need to be taken to the doctor for checkups. The doctor for animals is called a *veterinarian* and it is very important that he/she explains to you what has to be done so your kitten will not get sick. The veterinarian will also tell you about the vaccines your pet will need, the food you should give him, and other important things. The veterinarian will also answer any questions you may have about cats and recommend some books to keep you informed. You can learn a lot of things about your cat!

TEACHING A CAT

Sometimes kittens will scratch or bite you when they are playing, but you must teach them not do that. If he bites or scratches, tap your kitten's face *very lightly* with your fingertips, say NO! in a loud and clear voice, and stop playing with him. Do not ever hit him, shout at him, or mistreat him in any other way. If you do, your kitten might not trust you again and will not come back to you to play. Punishments should go together with rewards for everything the kitten has done well.

CAT LANGUAGE

If you look carefully, you will see it is easy to understand how your kitten is feeling. If he arches his back, stiffens his legs, fluffs his tail and his fur stands on end, it means that if the dog (or other animal) in front of him does not go away, he may attack. When your kitten is happy, he carries his tail up, the tip pointing forward and looking like a hook. When he feels like being petted, he swings his tail slowly, but if he whips it from side to side, it means he is very upset!

FEEDING YOUR CAT

Giving your kitten good food is very important so he will grow to be strong and healthy. Cats will eat either beef or fish. They also need vegetables and vitamins to maintain good health. That's why premium cat food is so good for them—it has everything cats need.

The best thing is to go to a specialty pet store with your parents. There, they will tell you which food is best for your kitten, how much food he needs, and how often he should be fed.

SCRATCHING

Cats usually leave scratching marks to indicate very clearly that a certain territory is claimed. Other cats will see the scratches and know that this house is already taken. But scratching is also useful to keep their nails (or claws) in good shape. The problem is that cats sometimes decide to scratch sofas, carpets, or chairs. To prevent your kitten from scratching where he should not, give him an old piece of wood or buy him a scratching post. You can find one at any pet shop. Remember, cats need to scratch!

COMMON DANGERS

Swimming pools are very dangerous for kittens, because if they fall in, they won't be able to get out. Sometimes, curious kittens climb inside open drawers and cupboards and end up locked inside until someone hears them meowing desperately. It is important to check that your kitten is not inside the washing machine! When you go to the bathroom, always leave the toilet seat down—yours wouldn't be the first kitten to slip into the bowl!

LET'S TAKE CARE OF OUR NEW CAT

First edition for the United States, its territories
and dependencies, and Canada published in 2006
by Barron's Educational Series, Inc.

Text and illustrations © copyright 2006
by Gemser Publications, S.L.

All inquiries should be addressed to:
Barron's Educational Series, Inc.
250 Wireless Blvd.
Hauppauge, NY 11788
www.barronseduc.com

ISBN-10: 0-7641-3452-3
ISBN-13: 978-0-7641-3452-4

Library of Congress Catalog Card No. 2006921562

Printed in China
9 8 7 6 5 4 3 2